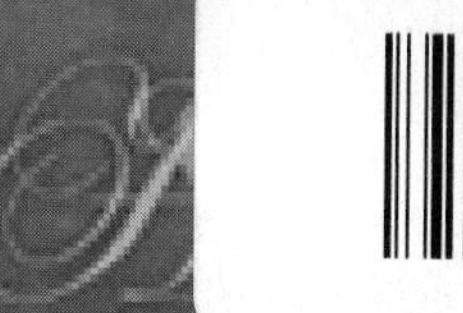

A Renewed Heart

VONETTE Zachary BRIGHT

NewLife PUBLICATIONS

My Heart in His Hands Bible Study: A Renewed Heart

Published by
New*Life* Publications
A ministry of Campus Crusade for Christ
P.O. Box 620877
Orlando, FL 32862-0877

ISBN 1-56399-176-4

Design and production by Genesis Group

Cover by Koechel-Peterson Design

Printed in the United States of America

Unless otherwise indicated, Scripture quotations are from the *New International Version*, © 1973, 1978, 1984 by the International Bible Society. Published by Zondervan Bible Publishers, Grand Rapids, Michigan.

For more information, write:

L.I.F.E., Campus Crusade for Christ—P.O. Box 40, Flemington Markets, 2129, Australia

Campus Crusade for Christ of Canada—Box 529, Sumas, WA 98295

Campus Crusade for Christ—Fairgate House, King's Road, Tyseley, Birmingham, B11 2AA, United Kingdom

Lay Institute for Evangelism, Campus Crusade for Christ—P.O. Box 8786, Auckland, 1035, New Zealand

Campus Crusade for Christ—9 Lock Road #3-03, PacCan Centre, Singapore

Great Commission Movement of Nigeria—P.O. Box 500, Jos, Plateau State, Nigeria, West Africa

Campus Crusade for Christ International—100 Lake Hart Drive, Orlando, FL 32832, USA

Contents

My Dear Friends

I want to welcome you to this Bible study series for women! I'm excited about the opportunity to walk through the Scriptures with you as we explore all that God's Word has for the busy woman of today.

Every unique detail of a woman's life fits into a grand and glorious plan. My prayer is that women of all ages will desire to have a deeper relationship with God, and to discover the joys of knowing Him and His plan for their lives.

God's Word speaks so directly to every aspect of a woman's life. It fills us with wisdom, imparts God's love, and provides ample instructions for our daily walk. The Scriptures tell us the results we can expect when we live in agreement with God's plan, and what we can expect if we do not live as He directs.

The Bible has much to say about its value and relevance for our lives today. It gives us guidance: "Your word is a lamp to my feet and a light for my path" (Psalm 119:105). It gives understanding: "The unfolding of your words gives light; it gives understanding to the simple" (Psalm 119:130). It is not made up of cold, dead words, but living, Spirit-filled words that can affect our hearts and our lives: "For the word of God is living and active. Sharper than any double-edged sword, it penetrates even to dividing soul and spirit, joints and marrow; it judges the thoughts and attitudes of the heart" (Hebrews 4:12).

When I wrote the devotional books for the series *My Heart In His Hands*, it was with the desire to encourage women and to help them realize that God is interested and involved in the details of their lives. My goal was to provide a practical and systematic way for a woman to examine her heart and recognize how beautifully God has created her. This set of study guides has been designed to complement each seasonal devotional.

Each study guide has been developed prayerfully and can be used for individual or group study. Perhaps you are part of a group that meets regularly to study and discuss the precious treasures of God's Word. I have been a part of such groups for many years, and I am still overjoyed to meet with these women.

Whether you will study on your own or with others, it is my heartfelt prayer that you will open your heart to His Word and enjoy the blessing of resting confidently in His hands.

From my heart to yours,

Vonette Z. Bright

How to Use This Study

The *My Heart in His Hands* Bible study series is designed for the busy woman who desires a deeper walk with God. The twenty lessons in *A Renewed Heart* embrace the glorious truth that any Christian woman can live a victorious lifestyle—no matter what life throws in her path.

A Renewed Heart provides everything you need to understand biblical principles and use them to transform your life. Whether you are working hard at your career, involved in full-time ministry, knee-deep in preschoolers, or raising teenagers, you can find the time to complete the short lessons and receive encouragement for your day. The questions require less time than most courses so that you can fit Bible study into your hectic schedule. The refreshing look at Scripture passages will help you apply God's Word to your daily needs.

You can use this book as an individual study during your quiet time with God, or as a group study with other women. (A Discussion Guide with answers to the Bible questions is located at the back of this book to help a group facilitator.) It can also be used as a companion to the *My Heart in His Hands* devotional series.

The book contains an in-depth look at the lives of two women: a biblical portrait of a godly woman and an inspirational portrait of an outstanding contemporary woman. These portraits, woven throughout the book, give insights into a renewed heart.

Each lesson includes these parts:

- His Word—a Scripture passage to read
- Knowing His Heart—understanding God's Word
- Knowing My Heart—personal questions to consider
- My Heart in His Hands—a timely quote to ponder

Whether to start your morning or end your day, you can use this study to focus on God's Word and on His marvelous works in your life. As you apply these principles, you will truly discover a renewed heart!

A Renewed Heart

As women, we sometimes allow life to overwhelm us. Whether as a mother of preschoolers who seem to need twenty-four-hour attention or a diligent worker who supervises complex job situations, we often have difficulty putting life into perspective. But God has a better plan for us.

If we look at the evidence in creation, we see renewal everywhere. A caterpillar emerges from its cocoon as a delicate butterfly. Barren trees, dormant in winter, are covered with buds in spring. Seeds lying under the cover of snow burst open at the first hint of warmth. Here are some other incredible examples of natural renewal.

A water bear is a little creature about the size of a grain of sand. These tiny bugs are found from the tropics to the Arctic, from the bottom of oceans to the tops of mountains. Whenever conditions become too harsh, the water bear reacts. If it gets too dry, the water bear shuts down its body processes and forms a sugar coating around its cells. It doesn't move, eat, or breathe. It appears dead. But when water is added again into its environment, the water bear "comes back to life."

Fishermen have harvested oysters for centuries. Years ago, fishermen would kill starfish (sea stars) because the aquatic creatures eat oysters. The fishermen would chop the starfish into pieces and throw the fragments back into the water. What they didn't realize was that each starfish part was able to grow into a new creature. What seemed like the ending of life for the starfish was actually the beginning of many more lives.

Creation displays what is so evident in God's Word—God's goal is for renewal. Even before creation, He planned for our regeneration through His Son, Jesus Christ.

We are like that water bear, encrusted by sin, dead to God's Spirit, unable to reach toward Him. Our lives are restricted by human limitations and spiritual death. We are helpless without God's touch. In His love, He reached down in the fleshly form of His Son, Jesus Christ, who died to make possible our spiritual regeneration. We were given the opportunity for new life, abundant and joyful.

When we place our trust in Christ, God renews us through the power of His Spirit so we can live above our sin nature and our physical limitations. We have a heart that is able to do all God wants it to do. Our lives are filled with righteousness and light rather than sin and darkness.

Paul writes, "This righteousness from God comes through faith in Jesus Christ to all who believe. There is no difference, for all have sinned and fall short of the glory of God, and are justified freely by his grace through the redemption that came by Christ Jesus" (Romans 3:22–24).

Our renewal is not merely a one-time event. It begins at our adoption into God's family as a new believer and continues through our spiritual growth until the day we pass from our earthly life into Christ's presence. Sometimes in a leap, other times inch by inch, we are transformed into Christ's image. The touch of God's hands reveals the sin hindering our growth, gives us strength when we are weary, and draws us nearer to Him.

What area of renewal do you need? Are you struggling with a particular sin, or feeling that circumstances have beaten you down? Do you wonder how you can find renewal? Do things seem hopeless? No matter how overwhelming the tasks of life may be, when you place your heart in God's hands, you will experience the joy of renewal and the hope of eternal blessings.

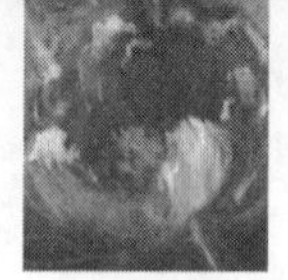

A BIBLICAL PORTRAIT

The Heart of Ruth

Romance novels sell in the millions and every month new releases fill the bookstore shelves. Unfortunately, many of the plots present an unrealistic scenario, leaving the reader with expectations for her life that cannot be realized.

The dramatic account in the Book of Ruth has all the intrigue and emotion of the most well-constructed plot. However, the story of Ruth is less about romance than it is about the character of God and His faithfulness to fulfill a plan for the redemption of the world.

Ruth, a Moabite, grew up in a nation that worshiped the false god Chemosh. When Ruth married Mahlon, an Israelite, she converted to his belief and honored the God of Israel. Her mother-in-law, Naomi, became her mentor.

In our culture, mothers-in-law have been the point of many jokes and are usually cast in a negative light. Ruth, however, appreciated her mother-in-law. Since Ruth was childless when her husband died after ten years of marriage, her mother-in-law became her source of comfort and understanding. As Christian women, we can draw from the example of Naomi and Ruth and make it our purpose to demonstrate God's love and acceptance to those in our extended family.

Following the death of both of her sons, Naomi's unselfish reaction was to encourage her two daughters-in-law to find a new life and marry again. One daughter-in-law decided to return to her family. However, Ruth, a woman of deep commitment, made it clear that she was not leaving Naomi. Instead, Ruth would leave her own homeland and accompany Naomi to Judah. Ruth's statement, a classic passage quoted in many marriage ceremonies, is the evidence of the depth of their relationship: "Where you go I will go, and where you stay I will stay. Your people will be my people and your God my God" (Ruth 1:16). The commitment between Ruth and Naomi is a model of a covenant relationship.

But the story has just begun. As you read the Book of Ruth, the romance of Ruth and Boaz unfolds with charming details. The inward beauty of Ruth was surely what captured his heart. A joyful, hard-working woman committed to the God of Israel and loyal to her mother-in-law, Ruth was honored by God and given a husband who adored her. Not only did she find in Boaz a "kinsman-redeemer," but she was also blessed with a son, Obed. He became the grandfather of David from whose lineage Christ the Redeemer was born.

Ruth's story shows how God not only works through circumstances to bring about renewal in our lives, but also how He works through godly character. If Ruth had not been loyal to Naomi, she never would have gone to Judah. She never would have met and married Boaz. And she never would have borne a son in the line of David. God brought a new and exciting life out of what initially seemed a tragic and hopeless situation.

Ruth represents for us the wonderful blessing of God on a life willing to break from the past and faithfully follow His leading. As you consider the life of Ruth, think about your relationship to Jesus Christ and the beautiful love that He not only demonstrated in giving His life for you, but that He shows with His presence in your life today. He will not disappoint you. He will provide renewal for every area of your life.

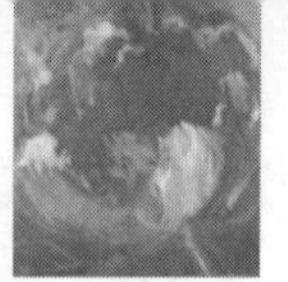

AN INSPIRATIONAL PORTRAIT

The Heart of Catherine Booth

If you had to name the most influential woman of the past few centuries, Catherine Booth surely would be in the running. She and her husband, evangelist William Booth, founded one of the most widely known and greatly respected organizations for assisting the poor and downtrodden—the Salvation Army.

To look at the heart of Catherine Booth is to see a woman who was convinced that women can and should play a vital role in the furtherance of the gospel. Catherine took advantage of every opportunity to proclaim the saving power of Jesus Christ. The renewing of lives, both spiritually and physically, was her chief aim. She helped her husband in his ministry to the poor and needy even as she ministered to the wealthy and empty. She once said, "There are broken hearts in the mansions of the rich as truly as in the hovels of the poor."

Catherine's walk with Christ began when she was "truly and savingly converted" at age 16. That day, the words of a hymn by Charles Wesley pierced her heart and chased away any doubts about her salvation. In 1851, she met William through her involvement in the Reformed movement. When he later was assigned to the Gateshead area of England, Catherine became deeply involved in all aspects of his ministry, teaching classes and visiting the poor.

In a controversial move, Catherine began preaching in 1860. She and William conducted meetings together, seeing many come to Christ. Soon, she began holding meetings for women, where she not only shared her views on fashion, child rearing, and adoption, but also commented on the social problems of the day and stressed the involvement of women in the church. Catherine helped spread the idea that evangelism should be allied with social concern.

It was Catherine's work with wealthier members of London society that provided the support for their ministry to the poor in East London. Her efforts also helped elevate women to places of responsibility and usefulness in their Christian lives.

By the grace of God, many lives were transformed through the Salvation Army. These were typically former drunks, thieves, prostitutes, and other notorious characters. Many of the newly converted unabashedly shared their newfound liberation in Christ with other lost souls. Not only did the Booths introduce people to the saving knowledge of Jesus Christ, they fed them through their Food for the Millions Shops, assisted immigrants, and found work for the unemployed.

The Salvation Army expanded greatly in the 1880s to include many other countries, including the U.S. Catherine continued her speaking engagements throughout most of her life. And she continued to develop organizations and services to help women from all walks of life. The Women's Social Services became one of the largest rescue organizations in Britain.

After a valiant battle with breast cancer, Catherine died in William's arms at their home in London on October 4, 1890. To the last moment her cry was, "A sinner saved by grace."

Catherine's life was focused on renewal—helping both the rich and the poor find Jesus Christ and providing physical help to the needy. Her vision is still being accomplished throughout the world today through the Salvation Army.

Adapted from: Helen K. Hosier, William and Catherine Booth: Founders of the Salvation Army *(Uhrichsville, OH: Barbour Publishing, 1999).*

PART 1

The Need for Renewal

The baby is crying, your son can't find his homework, your husband left without his briefcase for his early-morning meeting, and you just remembered there is a bake sale after school—and you don't have a thing ready for it. After you tackle each of these crises, there are all the other daily chores that must be done and a project for work that needs completion. On top of that, you would like to squeeze in a few minutes for a quiet time with God. The busy, hectic life of a 21st-century woman drains the spirit like never before. You are physically, emotionally, and spiritually spent. There are times when there is nothing left to give. These are the times when you need to be renewed by God's Spirit. The old must be made new.

Jesus frequently used parables to vividly illustrate a spiritual point. The parable He tells in Luke 5 is valuable to us in understanding our need for renewal.

Let's look at Jesus' words to the Pharisees: "No one tears a patch from a new garment and sews it on an old one. If he does, he will have torn the new garment, and the patch from the new will not match the old. And no one pours new wine into old wineskins. If he does, the new wine will burst the skins, the wine will run out and the wineskins will be ruined. No, new wine must be poured into new wineskins" (Luke 5:36–38).

What good would it do to be only partially renewed? How effective will we be if we try to put a "patch" on our old way of doing things? God wants us to be renewed from the inside out—our thoughts, our emotions, our bodies, our actions.

The process of renewal is called sanctification, and it should be our continual focus until we leave this earth for eternity in heaven. Without sanctification, we cannot attain the maturity God has planned for us. Our spiritual growth will be stunted if we do not take part in His renewal process. Our bodies and our spirits can become tired and weary. But as Christians, we have access to spiritual and physical renewal through the Holy Spirit.

We need to remember that we are not of this world, but we can look forward to the next one. The good news is that each step of renewal makes us more like Christ, draws us closer to God, and readies us for our future hope of glory.

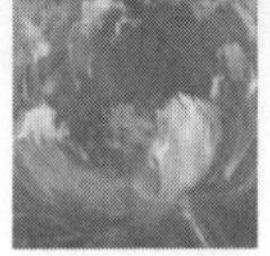

LESSON 1

No One Is Righteous

Do you have the same body shape as your neighbor, or the same hair color? Do you wear the same clothes? Do you make the same amount of money? Do you have the same outlook on life? Most likely, you will answer "no" to all these questions. But there is one common element that binds us all together: We are all sinful by nature. In our natural state, our inclination is to sin —to go our own independent way, to go against what God has ordained for our good. When we ask ourselves, "Why do I need renewal?" the first answer should be "Because I have a sinful nature." In this lesson, we will look at the words of Paul in the Book of Romans. Who does he say are the righteous ones? How should we view God's Law? How, then, can we be renewed?

His **WORD:** Romans 3:9–20

KNOWING *His* HEART

1. According to verses 9 and 10, who does Paul say is under sin?

   Who is righteous, not tainted by sin?

2. What are the characteristics of those who are "under sin" (verses 10–18)?

3. According to verse 19, what is the Law's role in our relationship with God?

4. According to verse 20, what is the ultimate purpose of the Law?

KNOWING *My* HEART

1. What does it mean to you personally that no one on earth is righteous?

2. What particular sins in your life come to mind as you read these verses?

3. If we cannot be declared righteous through observing the Law, why do you think the Law is still important in our lives?

4. In this passage, how does Paul address the need for renewal?

My HEART IN *His* HANDS

"He himself bore our sins in his body on the tree, so that we might die to sins and live for righteousness; by his wounds you have been healed."

—1 PETER 2:24

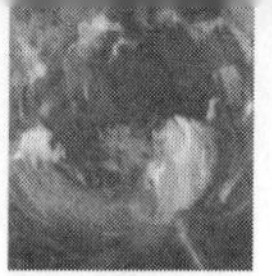

LESSON 2

My Human Limitations

When children play, they seem to have an endless source of energy. For them, nap time is a punishment imposed by mean adults who want to spoil the fun. As we get older, we find that having time to take a nap (or getting a full night's sleep) is one of the greatest pleasures in life. We tire more easily, yet there are so many things we need and want to do in any given day. Daily renewal of our physical strength becomes increasingly important. Isaiah had hopeful words for those who grow tired and weary. We can have strength that is beyond our human limitations, which will enable us to renew our spirits, minds, and bodies.

His **WORD:** Isaiah 40:27–31

KNOWING *His* HEART

1. What does verse 28 say about God's limits?

2. How does verse 30 describe our human limitations?

3. How does God help those who grow tired or weary (verses 29 and 31)?

4. What characteristics of God does this passage describe?

KNOWING *My* HEART

1. What are the situations in your life that make you tired, weary, or weak?

2. How can this passage help you during those times?

3. How do you feel knowing that God will renew your strength when you are weary and tired?

4. How can comparing your human limitations to God's limitlessness help you through a trying situation?

My HEART IN *His* HANDS

"To those who are sensible of their weakness, and ready to acknowledge they have no might, God does in a special manner increase strength; for, when we are weak in ourselves, then are we strong in the Lord."

—MATTHEW HENRY

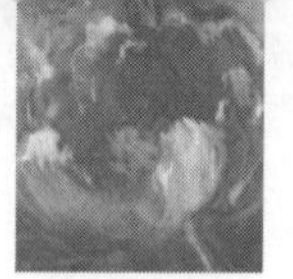

LESSON 3

I'm Not of This World

Those who have traveled a lot, especially internationally, know how it feels to be in a strange place. Communication is difficult, the accommodations are unfamiliar, and the routine is unusual. Jet lag causes fatigue and disorientation. After we become a child of God, our life on this earth can be compared to that of a traveler in a distant land. We are still in the world, but we are no longer part of it. This is not our home, although we live here until our Lord comes for us. Until then, God is working in our lives through the daily process of transformation—making us more like Christ.

His **WORD:** John 17:14–19

KNOWING *His* HEART

1. In verse 15, what is Christ's prayer in your behalf?

2. What is His reasoning for this request (verse 14)?

3. The word "sanctify" can be defined as "to cleanse and set apart for service." What is used in the sanctifying process and where

do we find it (verse 17)?

4. According to verses 18 and 19, why do we need to be sanctified by the Word?

KNOWING *My* HEART

1. What does it mean to be "not of the world" (verses 14, 16)?

2. Why do you think Jesus does not wish us to be taken out of the world?

3. We are sanctified, "set apart," through God's Word. How has following God's Word made you different from the world?

4. Are there additional ways you need to change to become "truly sanctified"?

My HEART IN *His* HANDS

"You, dear children, are from God and have overcome them, because the one who is in you is greater than the one who is in the world."

—1 JOHN 4:4

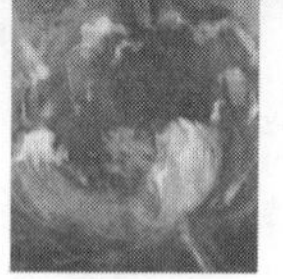

LESSON 4

I Want to Draw Near to God

We often feel most in need of renewal and refreshing when we are walking the furthest away from fellowship with God. In Old Testament times, Israel worshiped in the Temple, and only the high priest was allowed to enter behind the veil into the Most Holy Place to see the sacred ark of the covenant. The high priest could enter only once a year to atone for the nation's sins. By His death, burial, and resurrection, Jesus opened the veil and became our sacrifice for sin and our High Priest. Through Jesus, we became rightly related to God and have direct access to His throne. As children of God, our relationship with the Father is unchanging, but our fellowship can face times of distance. We need to draw closer to God, the source of our renewal.

His **WORD:** Hebrews 10:19–23

KNOWING *His* HEART

1. What does the "Most Holy Place" signify today (verse 19)?

2. In what three ways is Christ pictured as giving us access to God (verses 19–21)?

3. In verse 22, what has taken place in your life as a result of your faith?

4. What does this enable us to do?

KNOWING *My* HEART

1. Have you experienced times when you have felt distant from God? What were the reasons for this?

2. What circumstances are you facing that show your need to draw near to God?

3. When you are feeling guilty over a sin, how can these verses help you draw near to God?

4. How can you use this assurance to help you in the circumstances you listed in question 2?

My HEART IN *His* HANDS

"Thou has made us for Thyself, O Lord; and our heart is restless until it finds its rest in Thee."

—ST. AUGUSTINE

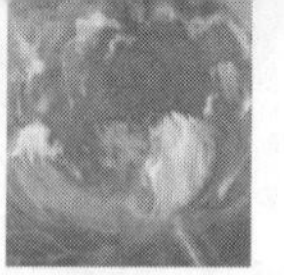

LESSON 5

Reasons for Renewal

When we look at the lives of prominent Christian women, we tend to see the successes, the end results. But we need to remember that they likely encountered the same things we do: they had needs, worries, questions, and problems. When we take time to consider what they went through, we can better appreciate what they accomplished. We don't come to Christ as perfect creatures; we simply come to Him as we are. It is through His Spirit working in our lives that we are able to walk through our circumstances and rise above our problems. Without Him, our sin and our human limitations would defeat us. The lives of Catherine Booth and Ruth reveal this need for renewal.

His WORD: Ruth 1

KNOWING *His* HEART

1. From the story of Ruth, describe her areas of need where she could use renewal.

2. What decision did she make that could have affected whether she found renewal? Based on what you read in the biblical por-

trait, what would have been the result?

3. What areas of need did Catherine Booth see in which people could use renewal?

4. How did Catherine facilitate renewal in the lives of others?

KNOWING *My* HEART

1. What touched your heart about the tragedies and trials that Ruth faced?

2. What hope can you draw from the ending of Ruth's story?

3. How does Catherine's life and service to others inspire you?

4. What specific actions can you take to help bring spiritual or physical renewal to others?

My HEART IN *His* HANDS

"The salvation of the soul is key to salvation of the body."

—WILLIAM BOOTH

PART 2

The Source of Renewal

Where do we find the source of true renewal? Throughout history, people have found innumerable answers to this question. In the aftermath of the tragedy of September 11, many people found themselves seeking renewal from their fear and terror. Tens of thousands of Americans turned to houses of worship to seek God's face for encouragement and security. James Ricci, a writer for the *Los Angeles Times Magazine*, posed an alternate solution. Although many of his friends found solace in prayer and communal worship, he is an atheist who has "wriggled out from under the burden of religion." So where could he go? Not a church or synagogue. He chose the Central Library in downtown Los Angeles where he spent hours reading about the Muslim faith. He was following his belief that understanding and knowledge will change humanity.

As children of God, we know how hollow Ricci's hope is. Education, knowledge, compassion, or any other good human quality can never eradicate our deeply embedded tendency to sin. Understanding our enemies will not automatically produce love for them. Learning practical steps to parenting will not change a distraught mother.

We must rely on the real Source for renewal—our God. He took the life of a murderer like Paul and transformed him into the world's greatest evangelist. He took the heart of an unknown foreigner like Ruth and gave her the opportunity to be the great-grandmother of King David.

What kinds of transformation have you experienced in your life? Have you discovered inner resources to deal with a family crisis? Have you reached deep for insights to resolve a sticky problem at work?

Aren't you glad that you don't have to run to a manmade institution for renewal? How comforting to know that the One who is always with us is our Source for every need. In the midst of a medical emergency, a financial upheaval, a personal depression, we can find hope and comfort. Our hearts are truly in His hands.

In the next five lessons, we will see how deeply God is committed to our renewal. Paul writes, "When the kindness and love of God our Savior appeared, he saved us, not because of righteous things we had done, but because of his mercy. He saved us through the washing of rebirth and renewal by the Holy Spirit, whom he poured out on us generously through Jesus Christ our Savior" (Titus 3:4–6).

Are you willing to go to the Source of renewal to find cleansing, kindness, and love? These studies will help focus your heart on the unlimited resources that God has prepared just for you and me.

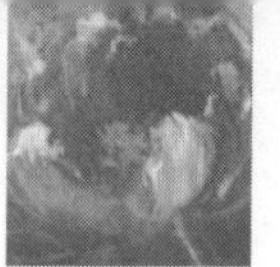

LESSON 6

Christ, My Savior

In Sequoia National Park in Northern California, the awe-inspiring giant sequoias tower hundreds of feet above the forest floor. From time to time, fires break out in this semi-arid region. Although we may view fires as a tragedy, they have a purpose in God's creation. For the sequoias, cousins of the famed coastal redwoods, there are two benefits. First, the fire burns off the top layer of organic matter on the forest floor, preparing the soil for seed germination. Second, the intense heat opens the tightly secured cones, freeing the seeds for new trees. Have you, like the sequoias, ever felt the heat from trials, or been "hard-pressed" from the challenges of life? In this lesson, we will look at the source of our strength during the trials of life.

His WORD: 2 Corinthians 4:7–18

KNOWING *His* HEART

1. When we are in the midst of trying times, what encouragement can we find in verses 8 and 9?

2. In verses 10–12, how are life and death related?

3. From verses 13 and 14, how important is faith to our hope for the future?

4. What should our attitude be in times of trial (verses 16, 17)?

5. What is meant by "what is unseen" in verse 18?

KNOWING *My* HEART

1. Which verses in this lesson would help you the most during times of weakness and burnout? Why?

2. When you've been "hard pressed," "perplexed," "persecuted," or "struck down," how did God's power keep you from being overcome?

3. How does the sacrifice of Jesus give you hope for your own renewal today? (Refer to verses 16 and 17.)

4. How can focusing on the "unseen" (verse 18) help you walk forward in this life?

My HEART IN *His* HANDS

"Your worst days are never so bad that you are beyond the reach of God's grace. And your best days are never so good that you are beyond the need of God's grace."

—Jerry Bridges

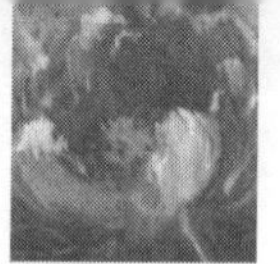

LESSON 7

Christ, My Healer

Are there areas in your life where you need Christ's healing? Do these areas weigh on your spirit? Christ is ready to heal you and change your life. In Luke 5:31,32, Jesus tells the Pharisees and His disciples, "It is not the healthy who need a doctor, but the sick. I have not come to call the righteous, but sinners to repentance." Christ does not expect us to come to him healthy, happy, and whole. He wants us to come to Him with our sickness, our sadness, and our pain so that He can heal us as no one else can. But beyond our physical or emotional ailments, the greatest area in which we need healing is in our spirits. Our sin is a sickness that only Christ can heal, from the inside out. Psalm 51 shows how this is accomplished.

His WORD: Psalm 51:1–12

KNOWING *His* HEART

1. In verses 1 and 2, what does David request of God?

2. What are the reasons David gives for his request (verses 3–6)?

3. Verses 7–12 list at least twelve specific actions that David is requesting of God. What are they?

4. How do these requests relate to Jesus and His work for us?

KNOWING *My* HEART

1. How do verses 1 and 2 encourage you to ask forgiveness when you sin?

2. Reflect on verses 3–6. Have there been times when these thoughts have been yours? What did you do about it?

3. Which of the actions in verses 7–12 mean the most to you in a current situation?

4. How can applying the truths of these verses help to restore the joy of your salvation?

My HEART IN *His* HANDS

"There is healing at the fountain; Come and find it, weary soul, There your sins may all be covered; Jesus waits to make you whole."

—FANNY CROSBY
"Healing at the Fountain" (hymn)

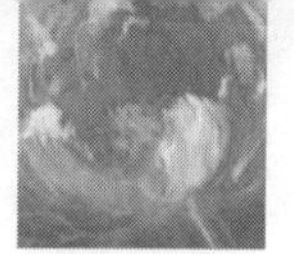

LESSON 8

The Holy Spirit, My Life

Computers have revolutionized our world. Our communication, our travel, virtually every facet of our lives has been affected in profound ways by tiny microchips. Data is transmitted, processed, and stored in an invisible, electronic form, but this data has become the control center of our world. We can't see the binary numbers as they go about their business, but we can see the results of their work, and we definitely can feel the effects on our lives when something goes wrong. For the Christian, the Holy Spirit is an invisible force, guiding and directing our lives. He should be our control center to help us accomplish God's will and to restore us when we are broken.

His **WORD:** Romans 8:1–11

KNOWING *His* HEART

1. Based on verses 1–4, summarize how believers have been set free from condemnation.

2. Contrast the minds of those living for the sinful nature with those living for the Holy Spirit (verses 5–8).

3. From verse 9, what should be the result of the Spirit of God living in you?

4. How does the mortal body receive life (verse 11)?

KNOWING *My* HEART

1. How does it affect you to know that those who are in Jesus Christ face no condemnation?

2. Think of a time when you let yourself be controlled by the sinful nature instead of the Holy Spirit. What was the result?

3. How could being controlled by the Holy Spirit improve your effectiveness in your role as a parent, at work, or in ministry?

4. How should the truth found in verse 11 change the way you approach daily challenges?

My HEART IN *His* HANDS

"No one has ever seen God; but if we love one another, God lives in us and his love is made complete in us. We know that we live in him and he in us, because he has given us of his Spirit."

—1 JOHN 4:12,13

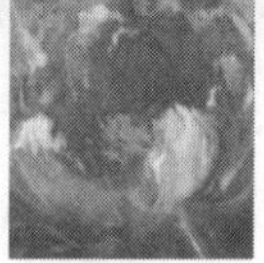

LESSON 9

God, My Father

Daddy, I'm tired. Will you carry me?" The five-year-old girl's little legs were tired as the family descended the long trail into Carlsbad Caverns. The father reached down and picked her up, positioning her on his hip. Instantly, the girl's world seemed much more bearable as the strength began returning to her tired legs. Like the classic poem "Footprints" tells us, at times we look down and can see only one set of footprints. But rest assured, God has not left us in these moments. He has seen how tired we have grown walking along in our own strength, and like any good father would, He picks us up—letting His legs be our legs and His strength be our strength. In Psalm 28, we will truly see that "the Lord is my strength and my shield."

His WORD: Psalm 28:6–9

KNOWING *His* HEART

1. In verse 6, for what does David praise the Lord?

2. What are the qualities of God given in verse 7?

3. How did David show his gratitude to God?

4. In what ways does God act like a father toward His people (verses 8 and 9)?

KNOWING *My* HEART

1. What problem in your life causes you to cry out for mercy from your heavenly Father?

2. Do you remember the last time your heart "leaped for joy" or you "gave thanks to Him in song"? What spurred your joy?

3. What do you think it means to have the Lord as your heavenly Father?

4. How have you seen God act as a shepherd in specific instances in your family? What did this mean to you?

My HEART IN *His* HANDS

"He is truly happy, whatever may be his temporal condition, who can call God his Father in the full assurance of faith and hope."

—BENJAMIN FRANKLIN BUTLER
U.S. Attorney General, 1833-1838

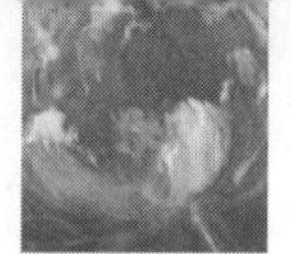

LESSON 10

God at Work

God works in different ways in each believer's life. One person is delivered from an addiction immediately at salvation, while another may struggle awhile and need the help of others to gradually eliminate the addiction. God may dramatically heal one person from an illness in an instant, while another is healed through the God-given skills of medical professionals. As we will see in this study of Ruth and Catherine, God may work in different ways, but He never changes. His ultimate goal never wavers. God is making us more like Christ every day. And He alone is doing it. We can't want it, will it, or work it out on our own. Only through the Holy Spirit are we made complete. Just as God produced spiritual fruit in the lives of these two women, He will use you to bless others.

His **WORD:** Ruth 2

KNOWING *His* HEART

1. How did God use Boaz to help Ruth?

2. What does verse 12 tell you about the source of the blessings that Ruth was going to receive?

3. What does Naomi reveal about Boaz in verse 2:20?

4. What was the source of Catherine Booth's enthusiasm for sharing the gospel and helping others?

KNOWING *My* HEART

1. Who has God used in your life to meet any emotional, physical, mental, or spiritual needs you have had?

2. What do you learn about serving others from the life of Catherine Booth?

3. How can ministering to others help in their renewal?

4. Described ways God has helped you in ministering to others.

My HEART IN *His* HANDS

"I preached as never sure to preach again, as a dying man to dying men."

—RICHARD BAXTER
English Chaplain, 1861

PART 3

The Basics of Renewal

As women, we have common examples of renewal at our fingertips:

- The sweet look of a fussy baby who has just awakened from a nap
- The fresh smell of the once-dirty little boy who steps from his bath
- The welcome plop of raindrops on parched garden soil
- The gentle feel of chapped skin freshly smoothed by a velvety lotion

Do you remember the last time you hosted a large sit-down dinner? After enjoying the food and the company, you face the daunting task of cleaning up the kitchen: plates stacked haphazardly; knives, forks, and spoons piled like pick-up sticks; glasses and cups stuck in every conceivable spot on the counters.

What a mess! But right under the worst of the disorder is the dishwasher. It's empty and waiting.

Dishwashers are amazing—they can gobble up the sludge of food with such efficiency and secrecy. Put the mess inside, add a little detergent, close the door, and turn the knob to "super scrub."

What a pleasure to walk away as the dishwasher gently chugs. Then when you come back and open the dishwasher door, a fresh cloud of steam perfumes the air. The plates can be stacked in order on their shelf, the silverware placed in neat rows in their drawer. The glasses and cups all find their places with a sigh.

Our spiritual renewal is a bit like that—like a former mess now put in order. Of course, we must cooperate with the process, allowing ourselves to be cleansed, giving up to God our bad habits, wrong thoughts, and ungodly desires. We must let God transform our good intentions to make them conform to His eternal ways.

The psalmist says, "The righteous will flourish like a palm tree, they will grow like a cedar of Lebanon; planted in the house of the LORD, they will flourish in the courts of our God" (Psalm 92:12,13). Renewal is such a mysterious transformation, done by God's Spirit in the secret places within us. Who can ever understand the inner workings of God? But we can see the evidence—an orderly life filled with joy, peace, and love. This new way of life is untouched by the turmoil of circumstances, trials, and the stresses of aging. Instead, we are protected from being overtaken by the world and enjoy the comfort of God's hands around our hearts.

As you study the Scriptures in the following lessons, expect God to produce that kind of renewal in your life.

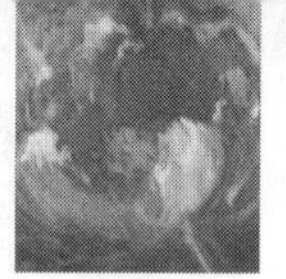

LESSON 11

The Eyes of Faith

"She looks at the world through rose-colored glasses." This is a familiar figure of speech. Someone looking through rose-colored glasses is an optimist; she views everything in a positive light. The deeper assumption is that we all have "glasses" through which we view the world. Our "glasses" determine our perceptions, which often determine our responses to people or events. These "glasses" are created by our earthly experiences as well as by our spiritual condition. Our "glasses" not only have a fundamental flaw—our sinful condition—but they also become clouded from the painful experiences we go through. In this lesson, we will discover the eyes that Christ wants us to have, that only He can give us—the eyes of faith.

His WORD: Matthew 9:27–31

KNOWING *His* HEART

1. In verse 27, why were the two blind men following Jesus?

2. How was the faith of the blind men tested in verse 28?

3. How did the blind men regain their sight?

4. In verse 30, Jesus told the blind men to do something. Why do you think they disobeyed (verse 31)?

KNOWING *My* HEART

1. Although you are not blind physically, is there an area in which you have some spiritual "blindness"?

2. If you took a problem to Jesus and He asked you, "Do you believe that I am able to do this?" (solve your problem), what would your sincere answer be?

3. What role do you think the eyes of faith have in spiritual renewal?

4. Think of something Jesus has done for you. Who did you tell?

My HEART IN *His* HANDS

"Faith expects from God what is beyond all expectation."

—ANDREW MURRAY

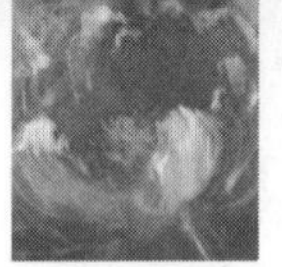

Lesson 12

The Face of Light

If you've looked at the face of a pregnant woman or a bride on her wedding day, you've seen her happiness and joy reflected in her countenance. She seems to have a "glow" about her. The light is not coming from an outward source, but from the inside, radiating from her expression to all those she encounters. If we can have so much joy over an earthly circumstance, how much more should the joy of Christ be reflected in our lives! Perhaps this joyful radiance is what Christ referred to when He said, "You are the light of the world...Let your light shine before men" (Matthew 5:14,16). Ephesians contains some practical ways that we can let our light shine on those around us.

His WORD: Ephesians 5:8–14

KNOWING *His* HEART

1. How does verse 8 describe the believer before and after receiving Christ?

2. Describe what we should do to "live as children of light" (verses 9 and 10).

3. How are believers to respond to darkness (verses 11 and 12)?

4. What effect will the light of Christ have on everything it touches (verses 13 and 14)?

KNOWING *My* HEART

1. Give a brief description of your life when you were living in darkness.

2. How does your life exhibit the "fruit of the light" as given in verse 9? How do you seek to know what pleases the Lord?

3. What do you think are some "fruitless deeds of darkness"?

4. What hinders you from living in the light?

My HEART IN *His* HANDS

"When the darkness threatens to overwhelm us, let us remind ourselves and others that Jesus is the light of the world."

—PRAISE AND WORSHIP STUDY BIBLE

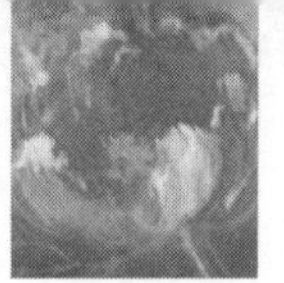

LESSON 13

The Garments of Love

Silk, wool, or cotton. Short or long. Small, medium, or large. Print, plaid, or solid. There are so many choices to make when we shop for clothes. Our appearance can be important in determining how people view us. Clothing is an expression of who we are—fun-loving and carefree or serious and thoughtful. Just like the clothes we wear, how we wear our faith determines not only how people see us, but also how they see Christ. When God adopted us as His children, He exchanged our filthy garments for pristine, pure ones. We are proud to wear His garments of righteousness. The Bible admonishes us to put on the virtues of Christ as we would clothe ourselves.

His **WORD:** Colossians 3:1–17

KNOWING *His* HEART

1. According to verses 1–4, why are we to place our hearts and minds on things above?

2. Verses 9 and 10 speak of taking "off your old self" and putting "on the new self," like exchanging ragged old garments for clean new ones. What specifically are we instructed to put off

in verses 5–11?

3. What new garments should we put on (verses 12–14)?

4. What are the practical steps given in verses 15–17 that will help you put on the new garments of Christ's love?

KNOWING *My* HEART

1. What is your mind set on throughout most of the day?

2. What old garments are you still hanging onto? What do you need to do to exchange them?

3. For which of the virtues do you currently have the greatest need?

4. How would your life change if you "let the peace of Christ rule in your heart"?

My HEART IN *His* HANDS

"Love means we value the other, even when that one is not loving in return."

—SALLY CONWAY

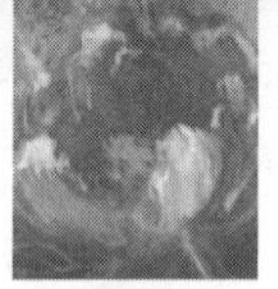

LESSON 14

The Life of Excellence

The Olympic Games showcase the elite athletes of the world —gymnasts, runners, swimmers, cyclists, skaters, skiers. Men and women train for years in these various events to become the best in the world. Excelling in sports requires more than athletic ability. It also takes passion, dedication, resources, and a lot of hard work. Excellence has its price, and those willing to pay it will rise to the top. God has a different definition of excellence, and the only thing required is to love. It is not enough to merely say that you love or to have the emotion of love; you must actively live out love as Christ has shown us. That is the "most excellent way" and a foundation to renewal. This may require as much patience and hard work as training for an Olympic medal. It exacts a payment of our emotions and time. This lesson will show us what it really means to love.

His **WORD:** 1 Corinthians 13:1–13

KNOWING *His* HEART

1. Although there are many good activities in the Christian life, why is love the most important element in all we do?

2. What are the characteristics of love (verses 4–7)?

3. Why is love more excellent than prophecy, tongues, and knowledge (verses 8–12)?

4. What qualities will last forever? Why do you think love is the greatest of these (see 1 John 4:8)?

KNOWING *My* HEART

1. Which of your benevolent actions are you performing without love?

2. In what ways does your love fall short of the ideal given in verses 4–7?

3. Spiritually speaking, are there ways in which you still talk, think, or reason like a child (verse 11)?

4. How does loving others help you grow spiritually?

My HEART IN *His* HANDS

"If we love, we can never observe the other person with detachment, for he is always and at every moment a living claim to our love and service."

—DIETRICH BONHOEFFER

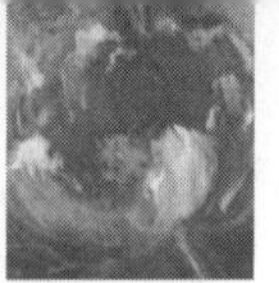

LESSON 15

Assurance of Excellence

In Paul's letter to the Philippians, he gives us this confident assurance: "He who began a good work in you will carry it on to completion until the day of Christ Jesus" (1:6). The salvation we received when we accepted Christ as our Savior is complete. But the work of sanctification has just begun. This is a process that is occurring each day and will continue until we go to be with Him or He comes back for us. Each trial, each success, each challenge, each accomplishment all work to teach us more about Christ and how to let Him live His life through us. The lives of Ruth and Catherine Booth demonstrate that this process takes a lifetime, but God is faithful to complete it. We are assured that He will be with us each step of the way.

His WORD: Ruth 3

KNOWING *His* HEART

1. What was the result Naomi was hoping for in chapter 3?

2. How did Ruth demonstrate excellence in approaching Boaz?

3. What qualities in Catherine Booth's life were evidence that she had eyes of faith, a face of light, and garments of love?

4. Both Ruth and Catherine lived lives of excellence. What qualities did they have in common?

KNOWING *My* HEART

1. What similarities can you find between Ruth and you? Between Catherine and you?

2. What qualities in these women do you aspire to attain?

3. Describe the transformation in your own life after you were "truly and savingly converted" as Catherine Booth was.

4. After studying these women and the biblical principle of renewal, in what areas of your life are you determined to live in greater excellence through God's power?

My HEART IN *His* HANDS

"If I want the Lord Jesus to be glorified in my life, I must run the race not to please myself, but to please the Lord—and that will often mean taking time to stop and put my arm around a weaker friend."

—Joni Eareckson Tada

Part 4

The Steps to Renewal

How can we continue the renewal process in the hard times as well as the joyous occasions? It is so easy to lose our way.

Once a young girl insisted on walking the ten blocks to school by herself. For months, her mother had accompanied her to school and hugged her good-bye. But now, the child had made up her mind that she could do it on her own. She was big enough.

She shouldered her backpack at her front door, hugged her mother briefly, then set off with her chin in the air. At the end of the first block, she confidently made a right turn and kept going. But as she looked back, a small stab of worry disturbed her as her home had disappeared behind the trees. At the next corner, her confidence wavered and floated away. All the houses looked the same. What had seemed so easy with her mother by her side now felt rather scary.

After a few more blocks, she knew something was wrong. She had never passed that snarling dog behind the chain-link fence. Where was she? Nothing looked familiar. Had she taken a wrong turn? And now a car seemed to be following her, coming up behind her slowly. She sped up her pace.

Then, suddenly, she saw the flash of dark blue metal from the corner of her eye. That color was so familiar. Sure enough, it was her family's car—and her mother was behind the wheel!

Her mother rolled down the window as she came alongside her. "Is your backpack getting heavy? Would you like a ride the rest of the way? It's such a long walk!"

The little girl let out a huge sigh of relief and a beam transformed her face. "Yes, I would!" she exclaimed as she climbed in. Her heart seemed as light as a helium balloon.

This is the secret to our renewal: We don't do it alone. God is with us—every step of the way. He knows every corner to turn, every bump in the road to cross, every strange, scary place we must pass. He understands our weariness, fears, grief, and hardships. He's there to give us strength, joy, peace, and power.

Aren't you glad that you don't have to muddle through on your own? We take each step in the presence of the God who spoke the universe into existence and who stooped to pay for our sins with His own Son. He is the key to our success.

The last five lessons in this study will give you steps to continue your renewal process: 1) Ask God for everything you need; 2) Search God's Word for wisdom; 3) Be still and wait upon God; 4) Determine to stay the course no matter what; and 5) Expect change.

Memorize these five simple principles. Then as you apply what you have learned in these final five lessons, use the steps as an ongoing process of transformation.

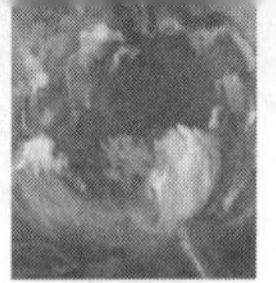

LESSON 16

Ask God for Everything

There's an old game for children called "Mother, May I?" in which players must ask the "Mother" for permission before making a move. This game teaches obedience and respect for authority, and children seem to love it. Although we don't need to seek God's permission to do every little thing, He does want us to talk with Him about the things in our day. He is a God of things great and small. Philippians 4:6 tells us, "In everything, by prayer and petition, with thanksgiving, present your requests to God." God has given us free will, but within that liberty, we can bring honor and glory to Him and receive His blessings for our obedience. God is waiting for us to ask Him—for anything.

His **WORD:** John 16:17–28

KNOWING *His* HEART

1. In verses 17 and 18, why were the disciples confused?

2. Describe the disciples' response to Christ's death (verses 20–22).

3. Compare verse 23 with 1 John 5:14,15. What promise do these

verses give and what is the qualification for answered prayer?

4. Why can we be confident that our prayers are being heard by God (verses 26–28)?

KNOWING *My* HEART

1. Can you think of an event that was painful at the time, but upon reflection, you now see that God had a larger purpose? Describe the circumstances.

2. How will these verses help you to patiently wait for answered prayer?

3. What hope can you draw from verse 24 to apply to specific issues or circumstances in your life?

4. Verses 26–28 highlight God's love for you. How does that help you continue to faithfully walk with Him each day?

My HEART IN *His* HANDS

"It is the answer to prayer which brings things to pass, changes the natural trend of things, and orders all things according to the will of God."

—E. M. Bounds

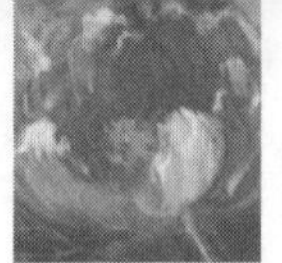

LESSON 17

Search God's Word

The apostle John writes, "In the beginning was the Word, and the Word was with God, and the Word was God...The Word became flesh and made his dwelling among us" (John 1:1,14). Jesus is the Word. Why do you think God is called "the Word"? One reason is that words are crucial in communicating His message. Without language, we are capable of living and feeling, but are unable to transmit our ideas to others in our generation or to the generations to come. Through "the Word" we learn what God is like and discover His will for our lives. God and His Word are inseparable. God's Word is important to our lives and guides us into the renewal that pleases God.

His **WORD:** 2 Timothy 3:14–17

KNOWING *His* HEART

1. What instruction for your life is given in verse 14?

2. According to verses 14 and 15, why are we to place such confidence in the things we have learned?

3. Verse 16 gives several characteristics of God's Word. What are they and how do they fit into the process of renewal?

4. What is the ultimate purpose for studying the Scriptures, as given in verse 17?

KNOWING *My* HEART

1. Think of people who have been instrumental in helping you to understand the truths of Scripture. How is your life different because of their assistance?

2. In what ways can you use the Scripture to help others become wise for salvation?

3. Describe situations in which verse 16 has been demonstrated in your life.

4. How could you apply the Scriptures to equip you in a specific "good work" you are doing?

My HEART IN *His* HANDS

"There are no shortcuts. If I am to grow, to mature, and to finally be transformed, I must feed on the Word of God."

—JOHN MACARTHUR, JR.

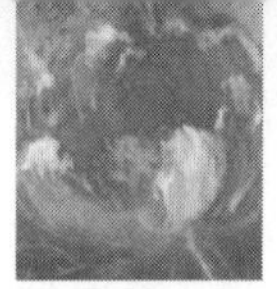

LESSON 18

Be Still Before God

New residents in Florida often say, "There are no seasons here; the weather doesn't change much." But there is a very important season—hurricane season, which stretches from June 1 to November 30. Those who have been through a hurricane know that the storm rages for hours, then the sky suddenly clears and the air becomes calm. But veterans of such storms know the worst is not over. There is more to come. The calm is merely the eye of the storm—the middle of it all. This calm is a temporary one. Those who know Christ and look to Him for comfort know that the calm and peace He gives are not temporary, but are authentic and eternal. This assurance of Christ's comfort is the reason we can "be still" in the midst of life's trials and "know that He is God."

His **WORD:** Psalm 46:7–11

KNOWING *His* HEART

1. Read Exodus 3:6. How does that verse enhance your understanding of Psalm 46:7?

2. What do verses 8 and 9 tell you about God's power?

3. In verse 10, why are we to "be still"?

4. Read Job 37:7,14. What is our responsibility before God?

KNOWING *My* HEART

1. How does knowing that you are praying to the same God as Abraham, Isaac, and Jacob give you hope for your renewal?

2. How does knowing that God has power to both destroy and bring peace affect your perspective on how He can help you overcome problems?

3. How difficult is it for you to "be still" before God? What can you do to deepen your worship?

4. What are the "battles" in your life? How can you rely on God as your fortress?

My HEART IN *His* HANDS

"Strength is often found within the silence
while resting in the presence of the Lord.
Abiding in his peace, we feel his power;
while leaning on his love we are restored."

—B. J. HOFF

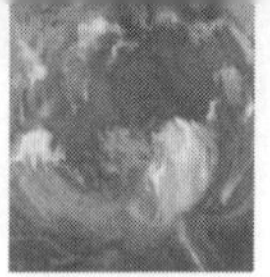

LESSON 19

Stay the Course

Adventure racing is a grueling sport. Teams of highly trained athletes hike, bike, canoe, and ski through hundreds of miles of the world's most challenging terrain. Each activity requires skill and teamwork, but the prevailing challenge is perseverance. The word "perseverance" means "not swerving from a deliberate purpose." Those athletes who reach the finish line do so because they did not swerve from their purpose of completing the race. Hebrews 12:1 says, "Therefore, since we are surrounded by such a great cloud of witnesses, let us throw off everything that hinders and the sin that so easily entangles, and let us run with perseverance the race marked out for us." How much more should we as Christians stay the course and cross the ultimate finish line, eternity with God in heaven.

His **WORD:** Philippians 2:12-18

KNOWING *His* HEART

1. According to verse 12, how are we to obey God?

2. How should we accomplish this (verse 13)?

3. According to verses 15 and 16, what will be the impact of

continuing to "work out your salvation"?

4. In verses 17 and 18, how firm is Paul's commitment to Christ and His people?

KNOWING *My* HEART

1. To "work out your salvation" means to continually grow and mature—working it out to the finish. What can you do to keep growing in your faith?

2. Why is it important to "shine like stars" in our world?

3. Paul faced many trials during his ministry, yet he was able to rejoice. How can you persevere in your Christian walk and maintain the right attitude?

4. What part will rejoicing play in your ability to stay the course through hard times?

My HEART IN *His* HANDS

"Consider the postage stamp: its usefulness consists in the ability to stick to one thing till it gets there."

—JOSH BILLINGS

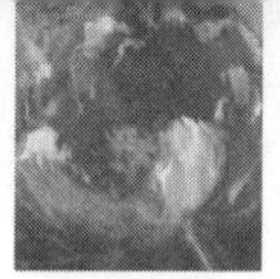

Lesson 20

Expect Change

Catherine Booth and Ruth led very different lives in vastly different eras. Ruth was a widow, a powerless position for a woman at that time. Catherine was a female evangelist, a pioneer in the Christian world who ministered to women of all walks of life. Ruth bore a son in the line of David and was a direct ancestor of Jesus. She didn't minister to a lot of people, but she did serve Naomi by remaining with her after their spouses died. Catherine was helpful in showing others to a place of renewal and regeneration through Jesus Christ. Ruth received renewal through her kinsman-redeemer Boaz. At various times, each woman was the giver or the receiver, the blesser or the blessed, but in all circumstances, God's hand can be seen working for good.

His WORD: Ruth 4

KNOWING *His* HEART

1. Describe the differences you see in Naomi's life between verses 1:20,21 and 4:14,15.

2. What are all the ways Ruth's life changed in chapter 4?

3. How do you think Catherine's life differed from that of other women in her day?

4. Describe the changes that happened in the lives of people touched by the ministry of Catherine and her husband.

KNOWING *My* HEART

1. Ruth's son is in direct lineage to Jesus Christ. Does knowing this change the way you view the beginning of the story? If so, how?

2. How might Ruth's life have been different if she had resisted change? How would that also be true for you?

3. How has God worked through crucial decisions in your life?

4. Which elements of Ruth's and Catherine's life examples would you like to apply to your own life?

My HEART IN *His* HANDS

"You cannot stay where you are and go with God."

—HENRY T. BLACKABY AND CLAUDE V. KING

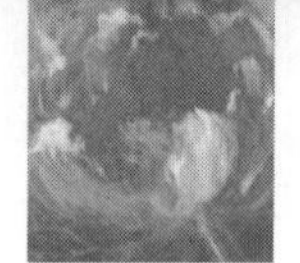

Discussion Guide

If you are using *A Renewed Heart* as a group study, the following answers to questions will help the facilitator guide the discussion. If you are studying the lessons on your own, refer to the answers after you have finished the lesson.

Answers are given for the first section of questions, called "Knowing His Heart." These questions are objective searches through the lesson's Bible passage. The second section, "Knowing My Heart," contains personal application questions to help you use the Bible truths in your daily life. Therefore, the answers will be unique to your situation.

If you are leading a group, discuss the first section more thoroughly, then allow volunteers to answer questions in the second section. Some answers may be so personal that group members will not want to express them aloud. Be sensitive to their feelings in this area.

The Lord bless you as you apply the steps to renewal in your life!

Part 1: The Need for Renewal

LESSON 1: NO ONE IS RIGHTEOUS

1. All Jews and Gentiles— everyone. No one, not even one.
2. They don't understand; don't seek God; have turned away; have become worthless; do no good; have deceitful and poisonous speech; are filled with cursing and bitterness; are murderous and full of misery; have no peace; and do not fear God.

3. The Law keeps us from proclaiming our own goodness and helps us see that we are all guilty and accountable to God.
4. The Law (the Ten Commandments) shows us God's holy standard, making us conscious of our sin.

LESSON 2: MY HUMAN LIMITATIONS

1. His existence is unlimited—He is everlasting (eternal); His power is unlimited—He created the ends of the earth; His strength is unlimited—He will never become tired or weary; His understanding is unlimited—His knowledge is beyond our understanding.
2. Even young people can become tired and weary, and can stumble and fall. No one is immune to physical limitations.
3. He gives the weary strength and increases the power of the weak. Those who hope in the Lord will renew their strength; they will soar and will not grow weary or faint.
4. He is eternal; all-powerful; all-knowing; He is caring and provides for those who hope in Him. He does not have limitations.

LESSON 3: I'M NOT OF THIS WORLD

1. That the Father would protect us from the evil one while we are in the world.
2. We need protection because the world hates us; the world hates believers because we have God's Word and are not part of the world's system.
3. Truth; in God's Word.
4. Because Jesus told us to go into the world but remain separate from it, we need to be saturated by the truths of God's Word so we can be effective and Christlike.

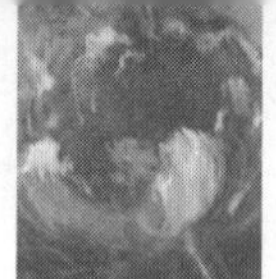

LESSON 4: I WANT TO DRAW NEAR TO GOD

1. The Most Holy Place is being in the presence of God.
2. He is the sacrificial Lamb of God who shed His blood for us (verse 19); He is the veil or curtain through which we pass (verse 20); He is our High Priest who atoned for our sins (verse 21).
3. I have been cleansed from my guilty conscience and have been washed with pure water.
4. Because our sins are forgiven, we can draw near to God with confidence, assured by our faith, cleansed by Christ's blood.

LESSON 5: REASONS FOR RENEWAL

1. As a widow, she needed physical provision, reestablishment of a family, a new home, and a new place in society through a family line.
2. She chose to remain with Naomi and her God, and not return to her own family. She would not have been privileged to become part of the line of Christ or experienced God's provision.
3. The lost needed spiritual renewal through Jesus Christ, and the poor and downtrodden needed physical renewal through practical assistance.
4. She preached the gospel whenever she had opportunity. She helped meet the physical needs of the poor by providing food, helping them find jobs, etc.

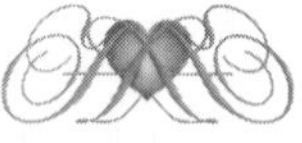

Part 2: The Source of Renewal

LESSON 6: CHRIST, MY SAVIOR

1. Although God allows us to go through difficult circum-

stances, He sets a limit. He will not allow the circumstances to break us.

2. Through Jesus' death, we can have spiritual life. By suffering for Jesus' sake, we are given over to death so that His life is revealed in our mortal bodies. Our persecution also gives life to the Church.
3. It is through faith that we believe and know that God, who raised Jesus from the dead, will also raise us with Jesus.
4. We should not lose heart, but remember that our troubles on earth are light and momentary compared to the eternal glory they bring.
5. God and our eternal life in heaven with Him.

LESSON 7: CHRIST, MY HEALER

1. To have mercy on him, blot out his transgressions, wash away his iniquities, cleanse him from his sin.
2. David recognizes his sin and that he has sinned against God. Since God desires truth in the inner parts (the heart), yet David had a sinful nature at birth, only God can cleanse him of his sin.
3. Cleanse me with hyssop; wash me; let me hear joy and gladness; let my bones rejoice; hide Your face from my sins; blot out my iniquity; create in me a pure heart; renew a steadfast spirit within me; do not cast me from Your presence; do not take Your Spirit from me; restore to me the joy of Your salvation; grant me a willing spirit.
4. Christ's death on the cross provided cleansing and forgiveness from sin. When we trust in Him, He gives us a new, pure heart and places His Holy Spirit within us. He made the way for us to have joy and a willing spirit.

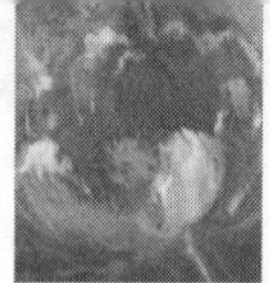

LESSON 8: THE HOLY SPIRIT, MY LIFE

1. According to the Law, the penalty for sin is death. God sent His Son in the likeness of sinful man to be a sin offering. Through Christ as Savior, we received freedom from condemnation.
2. Those living according to the sinful nature set their minds on the desires of that nature. Therefore, their minds are hostile to God. They do not and cannot submit to God's Law. They are controlled by the sinful nature, which leads to death, and cannot please God. Those living according to the Spirit set their minds on what the Spirit desires. Their minds are controlled by the Spirit, which leads to life and peace.
3. If you belong to Christ, you are not controlled by the sinful nature but by the Spirit who lives in you.
4. If Christ is in us, our spirit is alive. We receive life through God's Spirit living in us.

LESSON 9: GOD, MY FATHER

1. God has heard his cry for mercy.
2. The Lord is powerful, a protector, and trustworthy.
3. The psalmist found himself trusting in God more. He experienced joy and gave thanks to God in song.
4. He provides strength for His people and saves them. He blesses them and watches over them as a shepherd for all eternity.

LESSON 10: GOD AT WORK

1. Boaz protected Ruth by allowing her to stay in his fields and instructing his men not to touch her. He provided food and drink for her, and provided for Ruth and Naomi by having harvesters leave extra grain for her. He also asked God to bless her.

2. The Lord is the source of her blessings. Because Ruth had taken refuge under the shelter of God's wings, Boaz prayed for God to richly reward her.
3. Boaz was a kind man who, by showing kindness to them, was continuing to demonstrate kindness to their dead husbands. He is also a close relative, a potential kinsman-redeemer who can not only protect and provide for the two women, but can carry on the family name.
4. Jesus Christ. Because she recognized that she was "a sinner saved by grace," she freely shared the love of God with others.

Part 3: The Basics of Renewal

LESSON 11: THE EYES OF FAITH

1. They had heard that Jesus was able to heal people. They wanted the Lord to be merciful to them and heal their blindness.
2. Jesus asked if they believed He was able to heal them. They said, "Yes."
3. Based on their faith in Jesus, their vision was restored when He touched their eyes.
4. They were probably so thrilled at being healed that they were too excited to keep it to themselves. They wanted to tell everyone the good news about what Jesus had done.

LESSON 12: THE FACE OF LIGHT

1. We were once living in darkness, but as believers we are now living in the light, as children of the light.
2. We should exhibit the fruit of goodness, righteousness, and truth. We should seek to know and do what pleases the Lord.

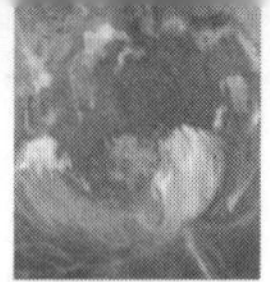

3. We are to avoid any involvement in the "fruitless deeds of darkness" and should not even dwell on what the disobedient do. We should expose them with the light that is in us.
4. Light exposes everything—the good and the bad. It is the light of Christ that will awaken those who are dead in their sins.

LESSON 13: THE GARMENTS OF LOVE

1. We should set our hearts and minds on things above, where Christ is, because our lives are currently hidden with Christ in God and we will eventually appear with Him in glory.
2. Whatever belongs to the earthly nature: sexual immorality, impurity, lust, evil desires, greed, idolatry, anger, rage, malice, slander, filthy language, lies.
3. Compassion, kindness, humility, gentleness, patience, forgiveness, love.
4. Let the peace of Christ rule in your hears. Be thankful. Let the Word of Christ dwell in you richly. Teach and admonish one another with all wisdom. Sing psalms, hymns, and spiritual songs with gratitude in your hearts. Do all things in the name of the Lord Jesus, giving thanks to God the Father through Him.

LESSON 14: THE LIFE OF EXCELLENCE

1. If what we are doing is not done out of love, then we are doing it for selfish motives and God counts the deed as hollow and worthless.
2. Patient, kind, not envious, not boastful, not proud, not rude, not self-seeking, not easily angered, keeps no record of wrongs, does not delight in evil but rejoices with the truth, always protects, always trusts, always hopes, always perseveres.

3. Prophecies, tongues, and knowledge are imperfect and will cease. Love is perfect (complete) and will never fail.
4. Faith, hope, and love. Love is the greatest because God Himself is love.

LESSON 15: ASSURANCE OF EXCELLENCE

1. Naomi hoped that Boaz would agree to be Ruth's kinsman-redeemer, to give her a home and provide for her.
2. She presented herself at her best; she was obedient in following Naomi's instructions; she avoided any appearance of impropriety; she agreed to follow the law regarding finding a redeemer.
3. She had a passion for Christ and His Word, compassion for the needs of others, concern for people to know God's love and forgiveness, and faith to begin a ministry that became worldwide.
4. Perseverance, love for others, commitment to God, selflessness.

Part 4: The Steps to Renewal

LESSON 16: ASK GOD FOR EVERYTHING

1. They did not know that Jesus was speaking of His death. They could not understand that He would soon die on the cross but then would be raised from the dead.
2. They will weep and mourn, in contrast to the rejoicing of the world. Their grief will be intense for a while, like that of a woman in childbirth. But their great joy at seeing the risen Lord could not be taken away.
3. God will hear our prayer and will give us whatever we ask of Him when we ask in Jesus' name and according to His will.

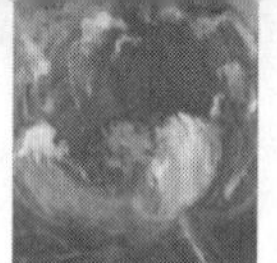

4. Because we love Jesus, the Father Himself loves us, so we can go directly to Him in prayer.

LESSON 17: SEARCH GOD'S WORD

1. Continue in what you have learned and have become convinced of.
2. Because we know and trust those from whom we have learned the gospel, and because we have studied the Scriptures for ourselves. They have taught us how to find salvation through Jesus Christ.
3. God-breathed—We must have God's power.
   Useful for teaching—We must read God's Word daily.
   Useful for rebuking—We must be open to changing what's wrong in our lives when pointed out by God's Word.
   Useful for correcting—We must be willing to abandon old paths for new ones that are illuminated by God's Word.
   Useful for training in righteousness—God's Word must become a part of our life through consistent practice.
4. To be thoroughly equipped for every good work.

LESSON 18: BE STILL BEFORE GOD

1. God is constant in that He was not only the God of Jacob, but also the God of Abraham, Isaac, and Moses. His magnificence is beyond understanding.
2. He has power over all the earth to desolate (destroy) or to bring peace. He can break both the offensive (bow and spear) and defensive (shields) tools of war.
3. To know that God is God and to focus on Him. He will be exalted among all nations on earth.
4. We must stop to consider God's wonderful works and exalt Him.

LESSON 19: STAY THE COURSE

1. By continuing to work out our salvation with fear and trembling.
2. By allowing God to work in us giving us the desire and the ability to fulfill His good purpose for our life.
3. As we live without complaining or arguing, we will be blameless and pure children of God. In the midst of an evil world, we will shine like stars in the universe as we offer the gospel.
4. He was willing to give all of himself, poured out like a drink offering of sacrifice.

LESSON 20: EXPECT CHANGE

1. In chapter 1, Naomi blamed God for making her life bitter and empty. She felt that the Lord had afflicted her and brought her misfortune. In chapter 4, her friends were praising the Lord for giving Naomi a kinsman-redeemer. She had a grandson who would sustain her in her old age, and a loving daughter-in-law who cared for her better than seven sons could have.
2. She went from being a widow to a wife, from gleaning crops in the fields to having more than enough, from being a foreigner in Judah to being part of a prominent family, and from having no children to having a son in the lineage of David.
3. She was fully involved with every aspect of her husband's ministry. She was also a preacher, speaking to large crowds of both men and women. She encouraged women to be more involved in church and with social concerns.
4. Many who were alcoholics, thieves, or prostitutes turned from their sinful ways and became bold evangelists, sharing Christ with others.

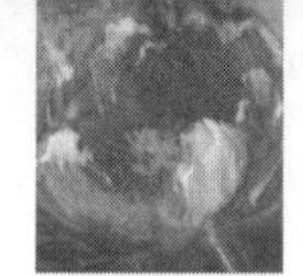

Beginning Your Journey of Joy

These four principles are essential in beginning a journey of joy.

One—God loves you and created you to know Him personally.

God's Love
"God so loved the world that He gave His one and only Son, that whoever believes in Him shall not perish but have eternal life" (John 3:16).

God's Plan
"Now this is eternal life: that they may know you, the only true God, and Jesus Christ, whom you have sent" (John 17:3).

What prevents us from knowing God personally?

Two—People are sinful and separated from God, so we cannot know Him personally or experience His love.

People are Sinful
"All have sinned and fall short of the glory of God" (Romans 3:23).

People were created to have fellowship with God; but, because of our own stubborn self-will, we chose to go our own independent way and fellowship with God was broken. This self-will, characterized by an attitude of active rebellion or passive indifference, is an evidence of what the Bible calls sin.

People are Separated
"The wages of sin is death" [spiritual separation from God] (Romans 6:23).

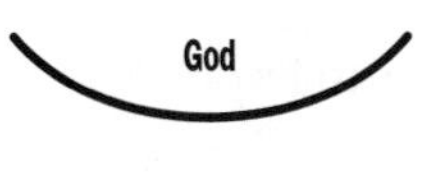

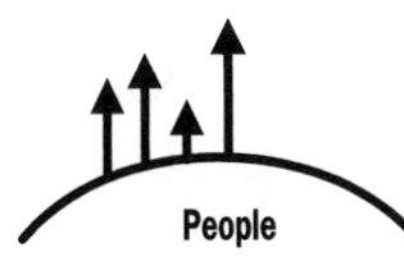

This diagram illustrates that God is holy and people are sinful. A great gulf separates the two. The arrows illustrate that people are continually trying to reach God and establish a personal relationship with Him through our own efforts, such as a good life, philosophy, or religion—but we inevitably fail.

The third principle explains the only way to bridge this gulf…

Three—Jesus Christ is God's only provision for our sin. Through Him alone we can know God personally and experience His love.

He Died In Our Place
"God demonstrates His own love toward us, in that while we were yet sinners, Christ died for us" (Romans 5:8).

He Rose from the Dead
"Christ died for our sins…He was buried…He was raised on the third day according to the Scriptures…He appeared to Peter, then to the twelve. After that He appeared to more than five hundred…" (1 Corinthians 15:3–6).

He Is the Only Way to God
"Jesus said to him, 'I am the way, and the truth, and the life; no one comes to the Father but through Me'" (John 14:6).

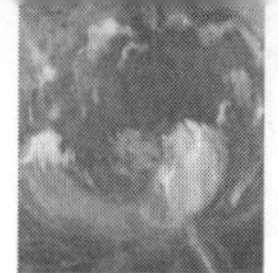

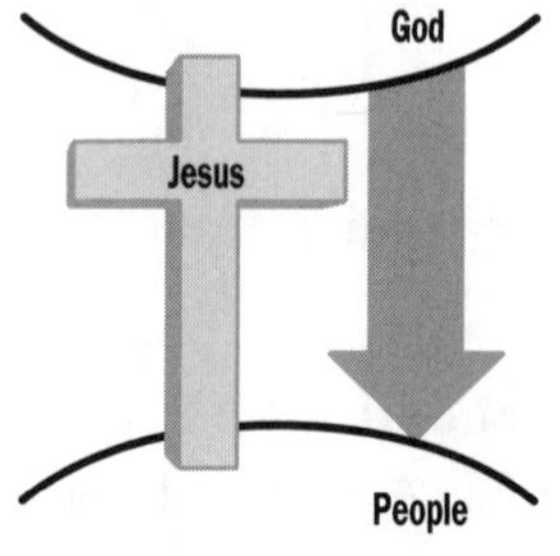

This diagram illustrates that God has bridged the gulf that separates us from Him by sending His Son, Jesus Christ, to die on the cross in our place to pay the penalty for our sins.

It is not enough just to know these three truths...

Four—We must individually receive Jesus Christ as Savior and Lord; then we can know God personally and experience His love.

We Must Receive Christ
"As many as received Him, to them He gave the right to become children of God, even to those who believe in His name" (John 1:12).

We Receive Christ Through Faith
"By grace you have been saved through faith; and that not of yourselves, it is the gift of God; not as a result of works that no one should boast" (Ephesians 2:8,9).

When We Receive Christ, We Experience a New Birth
(Read John 3:1–8.)

We Receive Christ By Personal Invitation
[Christ speaking] "Behold, I stand at the door and knock; if anyone hears My voice and opens the door, I will come in to him" (Revelation 3:20).

Receiving Christ involves turning to God from self (repentance) and trusting Christ to come into our lives to forgive us of our sins and to make us what He wants us to be. Just to agree intellectually that Jesus Christ is the Son of God and that He died on the cross for our sins is not enough. Nor is it enough to have an emotional experience. We receive Jesus Christ by faith, as an act of our will.

These two circles represent two kinds of lives:

Self-Directed Life
S – Self is on the throne
† – Christ is outside the life
• – Interests are directed by self, often resulting in discord and frustration

Christ-Directed Life
† – Christ is in the life and on the throne
S – Self is yielding to Christ
• – Interests are directed by Christ, resulting in harmony with God's plan

Which circle best represents your life?
Which circle would you like to have represent your life?

The following explains how you can receive Christ:

You Can Receive Christ Right Now by Faith Through Prayer

(Prayer is talking with God)

God knows your heart and is not so concerned with your words as He is with the attitude of your heart. The following is a suggested prayer:

> *Lord Jesus, I want to know You personally. Thank You for dying on the cross for my sins. I open the door of my life and receive You as my Savior and Lord. Thank You for forgiving my sins and giving me eternal life. Take control of the throne of my life. Make me the kind of person You want me to be.*

Does this prayer express the desire of your heart?

If it does, I invite you to pray this prayer right now, and Christ will come into your life, as He promised.

How to Know That Christ Is in Your Life

Did you receive Christ into your life? According to His promise in Revelation 3:20, where is Christ right now in relation to you?

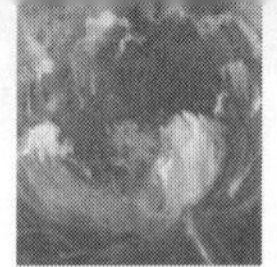

Christ said that He would come into your life. Would He mislead you? On what authority do you know that God has answered your prayer? (The trustworthiness of God Himself and His Word.)

The Bible Promises Eternal Life to All Who Receive Christ
"The witness is this, that God has given us eternal life, and this life is in His Son. He who has the Son has the life; he who does not have the Son of God does not have the life. These things I have written to you who believe in the name of the Son of God, in order that you may know that you have eternal life" (1 John 5:11–13).

Thank God often that Christ is in your life and that He will never leave you (Hebrews 13:5). You can know on the basis of His promise that Christ lives in you and that you have eternal life from the very moment you invite Him in. He will not deceive you.

An important reminder…

Feelings Can Be Unreliable
You might have expectations about how you should feel after placing your trust in Christ. While feelings are important, they are unreliable indicators of your sincerity or the trustworthiness of God's promise. Our feelings change easily, but God's Word and His character remain constant. This illustration shows the relationship among **fact** (God and His Word), **faith** (our trust in God and His Word), and our **feelings**.

Fact: The chair is strong enough to support you.

Faith: You believe this chair will support you, so you sit in it.

Feeling: You may or may not feel comfortable in this chair, but it continues to support you.

The promise of God's Word, the Bible—not our feelings—is our authority. The Christian lives by faith (trust) in the trustworthiness of God Himself and His Word.

Now That You Have Entered Into a Personal Relationship With Christ

The moment you received Christ by faith, as an act of your will, many things happened, including the following:

- Christ came into your life (Revelation 3:20; Colossians 1:27).
- Your sins were forgiven (Colossians 1:14).
- You became a child of God (John 1:12).
- You received eternal life (John 5:24).
- You began the great adventure for which God created you (John 10:10; 2 Corinthians 5:17; 1 Thessalonians 5:18).

Can you think of anything more wonderful that could happen to you than entering into a personal relationship with Jesus Christ? Would you like to thank God in prayer right now for what He has done for you? By thanking God, you demonstrate your faith.

To enjoy your new relationship with God...

Suggestions for Christian Growth

Spiritual growth results from trusting Jesus Christ. "The righteous man shall live by faith" (Galatians 3:11). A life of faith will enable you to trust God increasingly with every detail of your life, and to practice the following:

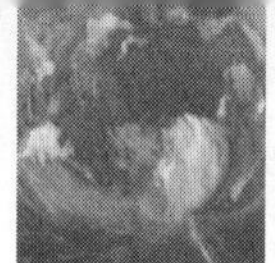

G *Go* to God in prayer daily (John 15:7).

R *Read* God's Word daily (Acts 17:11); begin with the Gospel of John.

O *Obey* God moment by moment (John 14:21).

W *Witness* for Christ by your life and words (Matthew 4:19; John 15:8).

T *Trust* God for every detail of your life (1 Peter 5:7).

H *Holy Spirit*—allow Him to control and empower your daily life and witness (Galatians 5:16,17; Acts 1:8; Ephesians 5:18).

Fellowship in a Good Church

God's Word admonishes us not to forsake "the assembling of ourselves together" (Hebrews 10:25). Several logs burn brightly together, but put one aside on the cold hearth and the fire goes out. So it is with your relationship with other Christians. If you do not belong to a church, do not wait to be invited. Take the initiative; call the pastor of a nearby church where Christ is honored and His Word is preached. Start this week, and make plans to attend regularly.

Resources

My Heart in His Hands: Renew a Steadfast Spirit Within Me. Spring—renewal is everywhere; we are reminded to cry out to God, "Renew a steadfast spirit within me." The first of four books in Vonette Bright's devotional series, this book will give fresh spiritual vision and hope to women of all ages. ISBN 1-56399-161-6

My Heart in His Hands: Set Me Free Indeed. Summer—a time of freedom. Are there bonds that keep you from God's best? With this devotional, a few moments daily can help you draw closer to the One who gives true freedom. This is the second of four in the devotional series. ISBN 1-56399-162-4

My Heart in His Hands: I Delight Greatly in My Lord. Do you stop to appreciate the blessings God has given you? Spend time delighting in God with book three in this devotional series. ISBN 1-56399-163-2

My Heart in His Hands: Lead Me in the Way Everlasting. We all need guidance, and God is the ultimate leader. These daily moments with God will help you to rely on His leadership. The final in the four-book devotional series. ISBN 1-56399-164-0

My Heart in His Hands: Bible Study Guides. Designed to complement the four devotional books in this series, the Bible Study Guides allow a woman to examine God's Word and gain perspective on the issues that touch her life. Each study highlights a biblical character and includes an inspirational portrait

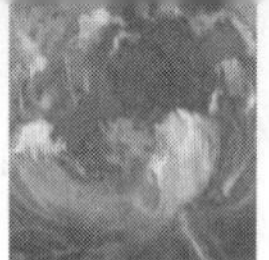

of a woman who served God. Available in 2002:
A Renewed Heart (1-56399-176-4)
A Nurturing Heart (1-56399-177-2)
A Woman's Heart (1-56399-178-0)
A Free Heart (1-56399-179-9)
A Wise Heart (1-56399-180-2)
A Caring Heart (1-56399-181-0)

The Joy of Hospitality: Fun Ideas for Evangelistic Entertaining. Co-written with Barbara Ball, this practical book tells how to share your faith through hosting barbecues, coffees, holiday parties, and other events in your home. ISBN 1-56399-057-1

The Joy of Hospitality Cookbook. Filled with uplifting scriptures and quotations, this cookbook contains hundreds of delicious recipes, hospitality tips, sample menus, and family traditions that are sure to make your entertaining a memorable and eternal success. Co-written with Barbara Ball. ISBN 1-56399-077-6

The Greatest Lesson I've Ever Learned. In this treasury of inspiring, real-life experiences, twenty-three prominent women of faith share their "greatest lessons." Does God have faith- and character-building lessons for you in their rich, heart-warming stories? ISBN 1-56399-085-7

Beginning Your Journey of Joy. This adaptation of the *Four Spiritual Laws* speaks in the language of today's women and offers a slightly feminine approach to sharing God's love with your neighbors, friends, and family members. ISBN 1-56399-093-8

These and other fine products from *New**Life*** Publications are available from your favorite bookseller or by calling (800) 235-7255 (within U.S.) or (407) 826-2145, or by visiting www.newlifepubs.com.